CAN YOU ARRANGE THESE NUMBERS IN ASCENDING AND DESCENDING ORDER?

MATH BOOKS FIRST GRADE
CHILDREN'S MATH BOOKS

BABY PROFESSOR
EDUCATION KIDS

Speedy Publishing LLC
40 E. Main St. #1156
Newark, DE 19711
www.speedypublishing.com

Ordering Numbers

Let's cut and paste the numbers in Ascending order with the Choo-Choo Train!

Cut and Paste 1

Arrange the numbers from least to greatest.

A 18 10 19 20

B 11 12 13 15

Cut and paste the numbers into the correct wagon.

18	10	19	20
11	12	13	15

For cutting purposes

Cut and Paste 2

Arrange the numbers from least to greatest.

A 14 16 17 12

B 15 11 14 18

Cut and paste the numbers into the correct wagon.

14	16	17	12
15	11	14	18

For cutting purposes

Cut and Paste 3

Arrange the numbers from least to greatest.

A 13 16 20 17

B 19 10 13 14

Cut and paste the numbers into the correct wagon.

13	16	20	17
19	10	13	14

For cutting purposes

Cut and Paste 4

Arrange the numbers from least to greatest.

A 19 20 10 15

B 16 12 17 18

Cut and paste the numbers into the correct wagon.

19	20	10	15
16	12	17	18

For cutting purposes

Cut and Paste 5

Arrange the numbers from least to greatest.

A 11 18 16 10

B 11 13 17 19

Cut and paste the numbers into the correct wagon.

11	18	16	10
11	13	17	19

For cutting purposes

Cut and Paste 6

Arrange the numbers from least to greatest.

A 12 15 20 14

B 14 11 16 15

Cut and paste the numbers into the correct wagon.

12	15	20	14
14	11	16	15

For cutting purposes

Cut and Paste 7

Arrange the numbers from least to greatest.

A 14 5 20 18

B 16 9 2 1

Cut and paste the numbers into the correct wagon.

14	5	20	18
16	9	2	1

For cutting purposes

Cut and Paste 8

Arrange the numbers from least to greatest.

A 15 3 6 4

B 10 7 8 11

Cut and paste the numbers into the correct wagon.

For cutting purposes

Cut and Paste 9

Arrange the numbers from least to greatest.

A 12 13 17 19

B 4 10 11 16

Cut and paste the numbers into the correct wagon.

12	13	17	19
4	10	11	16

For cutting purposes

Let's cut and paste the numbers in Descending order with the Choo-Choo Train!

For cutting purposes

Cut and Paste 10

Arrange the numbers from greatest to least.

A 13 11 18 12

B 16 14 15 17

Cut and paste the numbers into the correct wagon.

13	11	18	12
16	14	15	17

For cutting purposes

Cut and Paste 11

Arrange the numbers from greatest to least.

A 20 19 10 13

B 16 11 12 18

Cut and paste the numbers into the correct wagon.

20	19	10	13
16	11	12	18

For cutting purposes

Cut and Paste 12

Arrange the numbers from greatest to least.

A 19 10 17 15

B 20 14 12 16

Cut and paste the numbers into the correct wagon.

19	10	17	15
20	14	12	16

For cutting purposes

Cut and Paste 13

Arrange the numbers from greatest to least.

A 10 17 13 18

B 19 20 14 11

Cut and paste the numbers into the correct wagon.

10	17	13	18
19	20	14	11

For cutting purposes

Cut and Paste 14

Arrange the numbers from greatest to least.

A 15 16 11 17

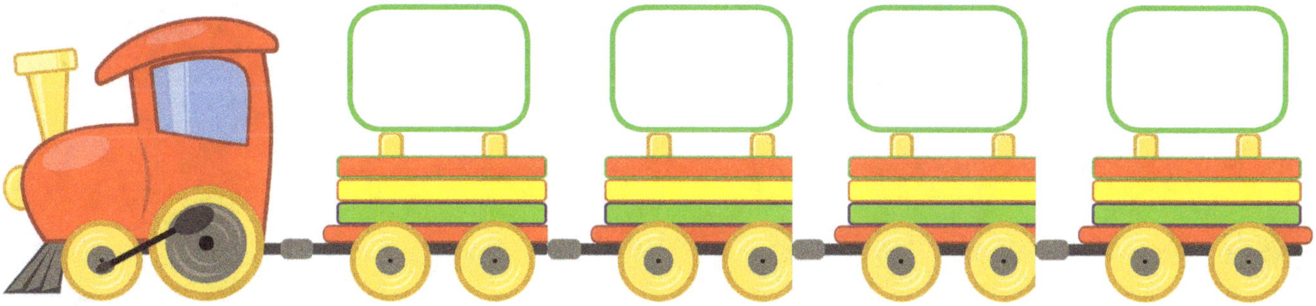

B 13 18 19 20

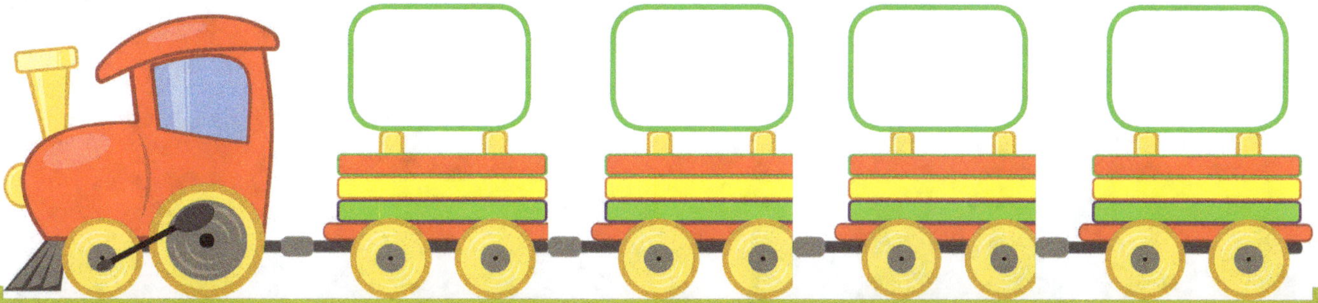

Cut and paste the numbers into the correct wagon.

15	16	11	17
13	18	19	20

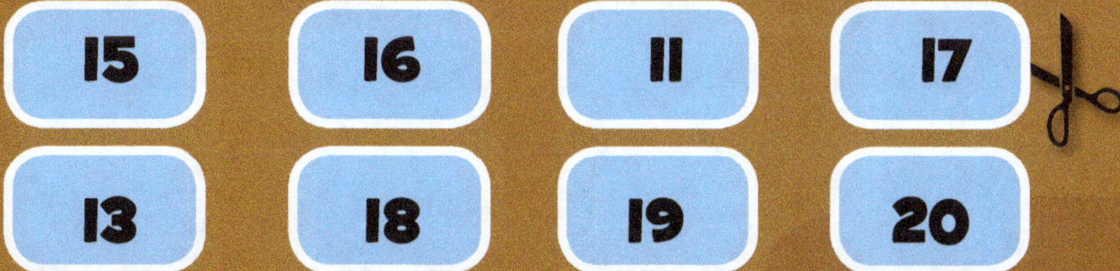

For cutting purposes

Cut and Paste 15

Arrange the numbers from greatest to least.

A 10 12 14 15

B 12 16 18 10

Cut and paste the numbers into the correct wagon.

10	12	14	15
12	16	18	10

For cutting purposes

Cut and Paste 16

Arrange the numbers from greatest to least.

A 12 3 6 13

B 1 15 14 16

Cut and paste the numbers into the correct wagon.

12	3	6	13
1	15	14	16

For cutting purposes

Cut and Paste 17

Arrange the numbers from greatest to least.

A 17 18 9 19

B 20 4 5 10

Cut and paste the numbers into the correct wagon.

17	18	9	19
20	4	5	10

For cutting purposes

Cut and Paste 18

Arrange the numbers from greatest to least.

A 7 11 2 8

B 5 20 6 16

Cut and paste the numbers into the correct wagon.

7	11	2	8
5	20	6	16

For cutting purposes

Let's arrange and write the numbers with the Choo-Choo Train!

Arrange and write 1

Write the numbers from least to greatest.

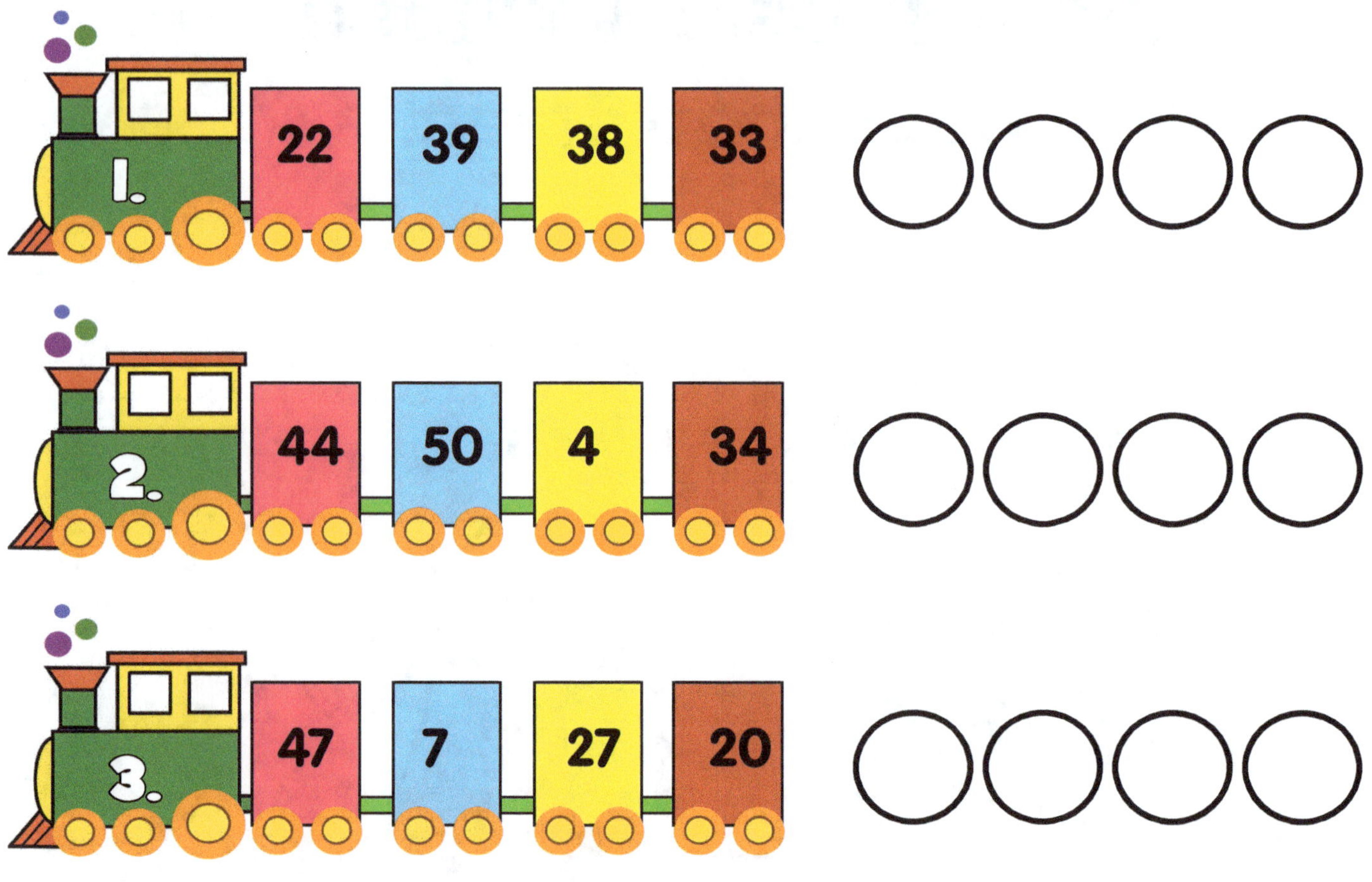

Name:______________________________ Score: __________

Arrange and write 2

Write the numbers from least to greatest.

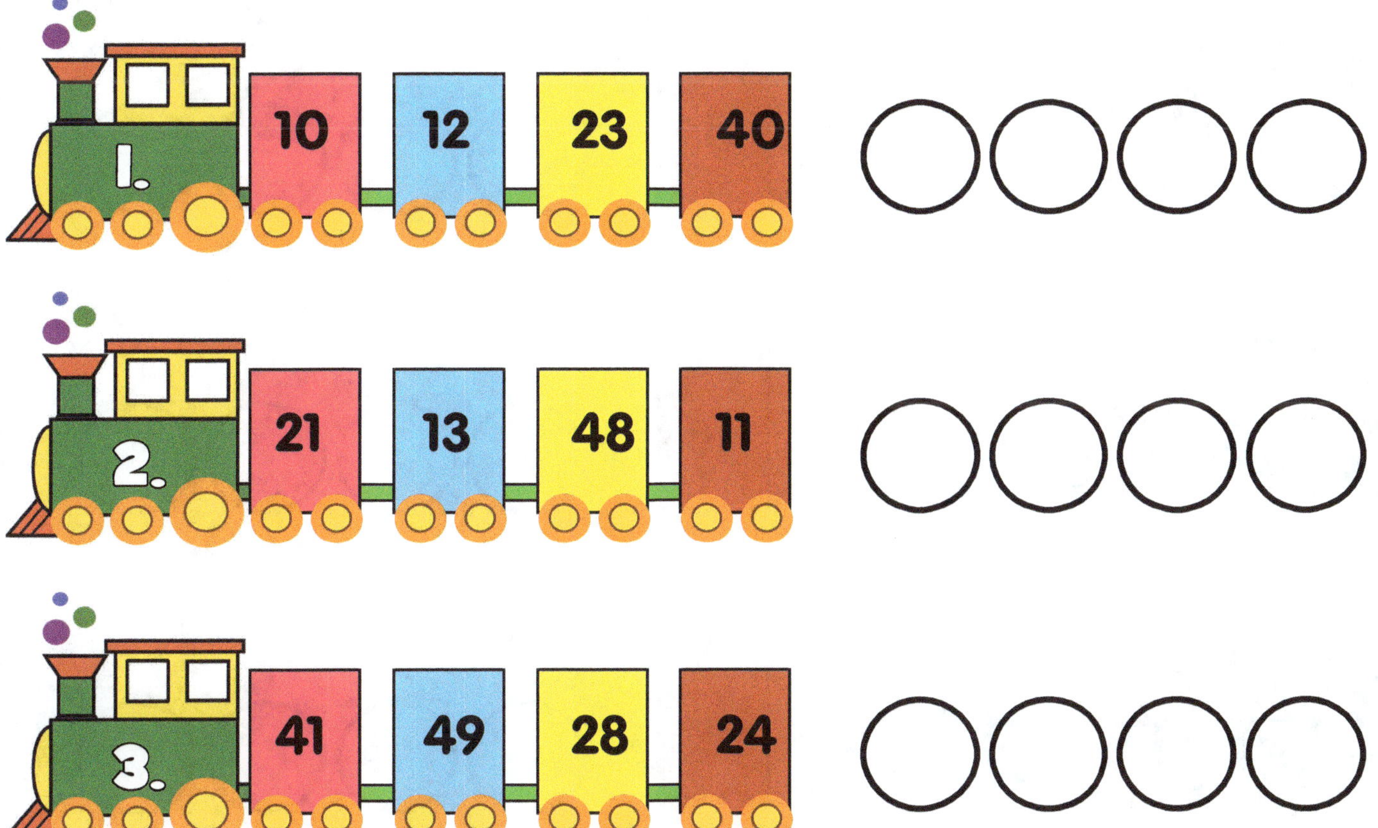

Name:______________________________ Score: __________

Arrange and write 3

123

Write the numbers from least to greatest.

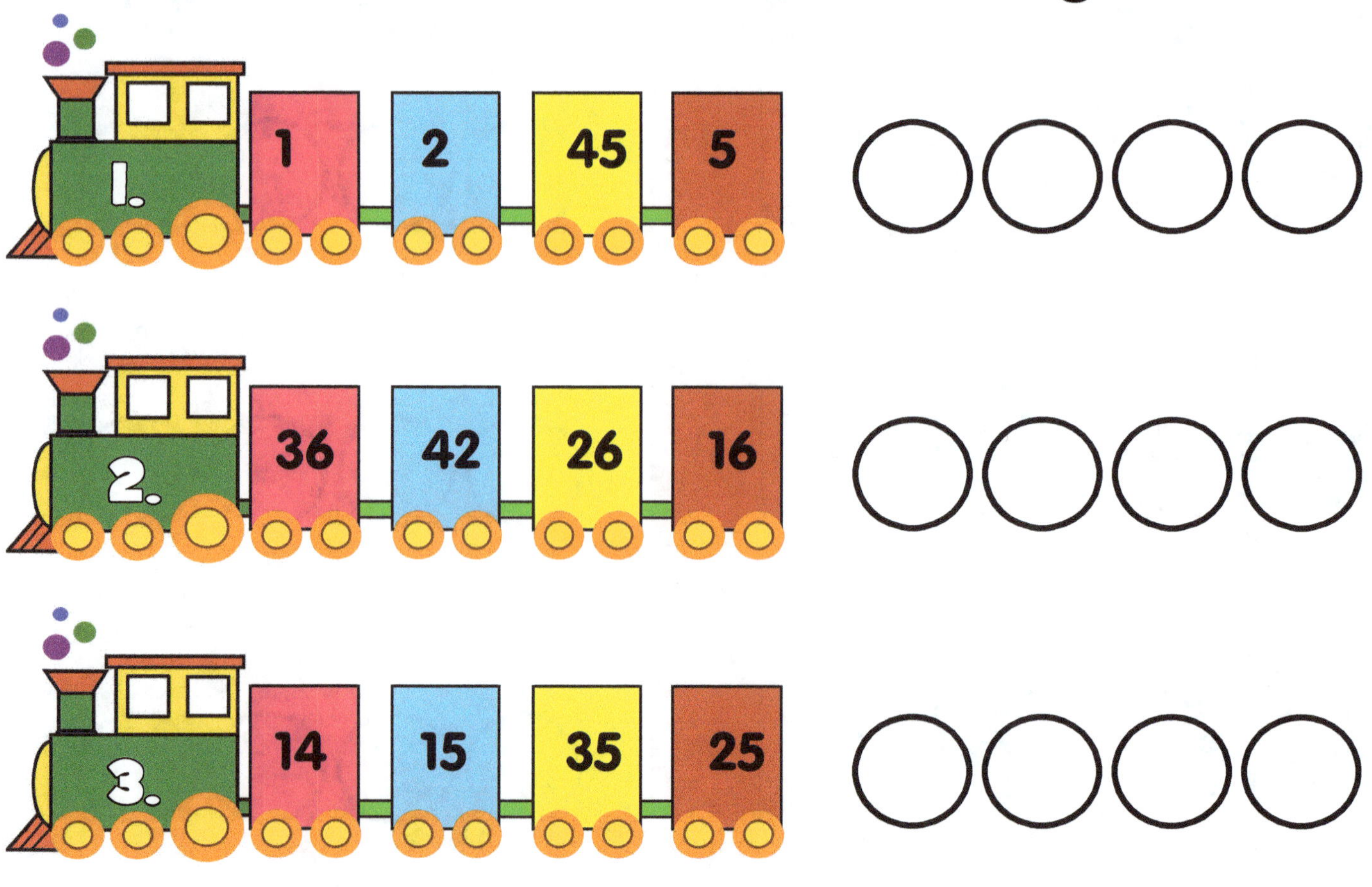

Name:_________________________________ Score: __________

Arrange and write 4

Write the numbers from least to greatest.

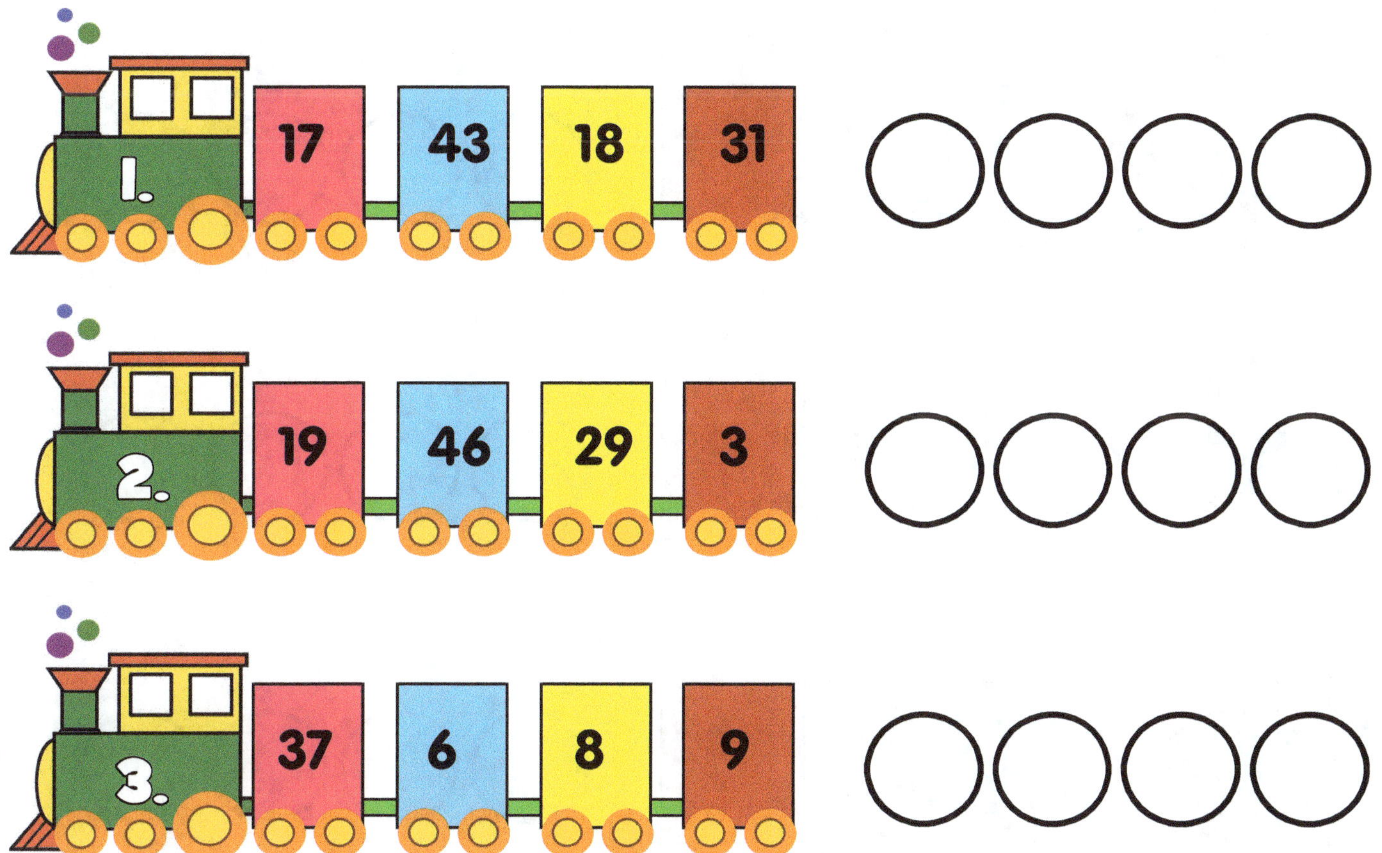

Name:______________________________ Score: __________

Arrange and write 5

Write the numbers from least to greatest.

1. 3 9 33 49 ◯ ◯ ◯ ◯

2. 20 15 18 45 ◯ ◯ ◯ ◯

3. 17 46 22 42 ◯ ◯ ◯ ◯

Name: ______________________________ Score: __________

Arrange and write 6

123

Write the numbers from least to greatest.

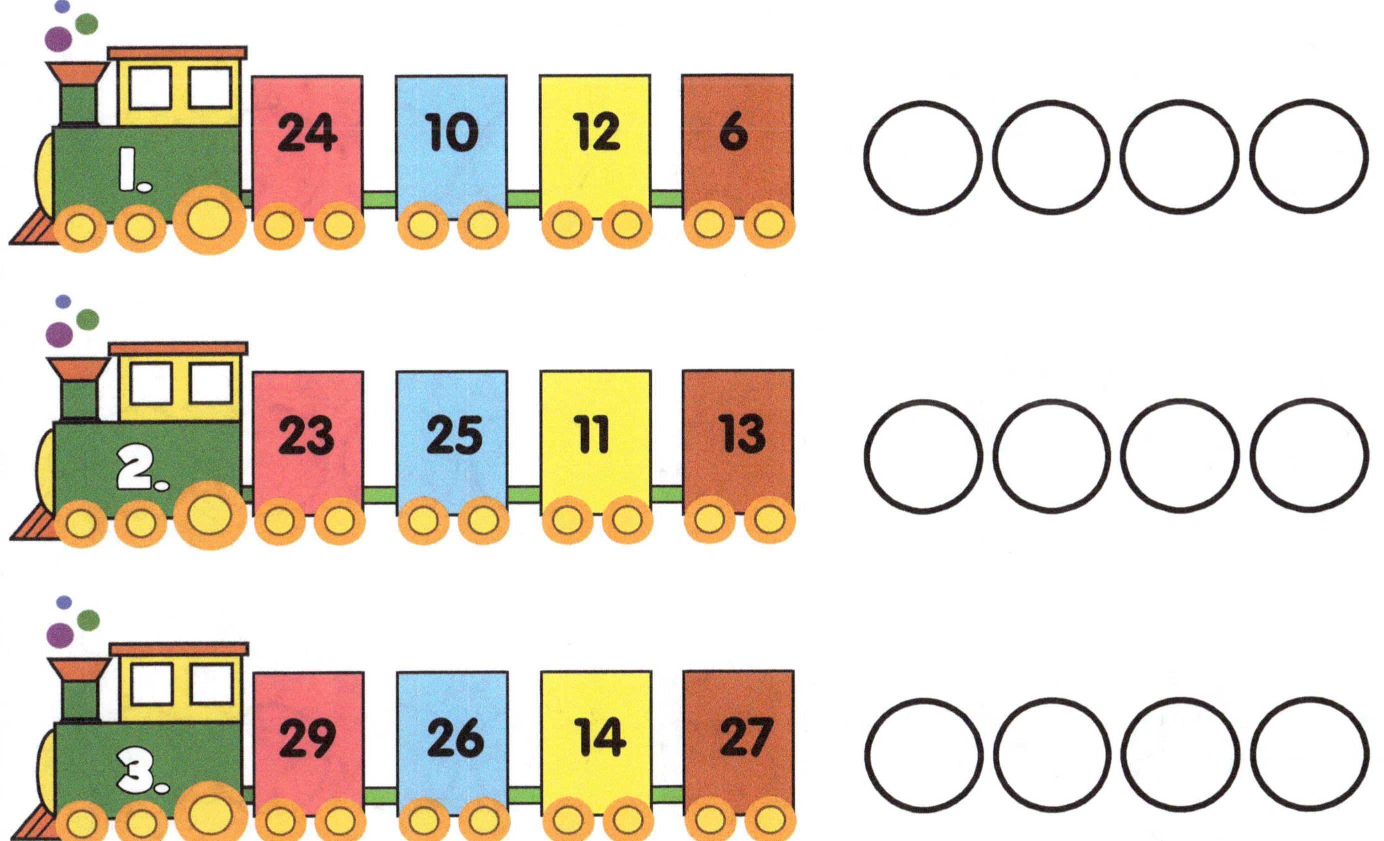

Name:______________________________ Score: __________

Arrange and write 7

Write the numbers from greatest to least.

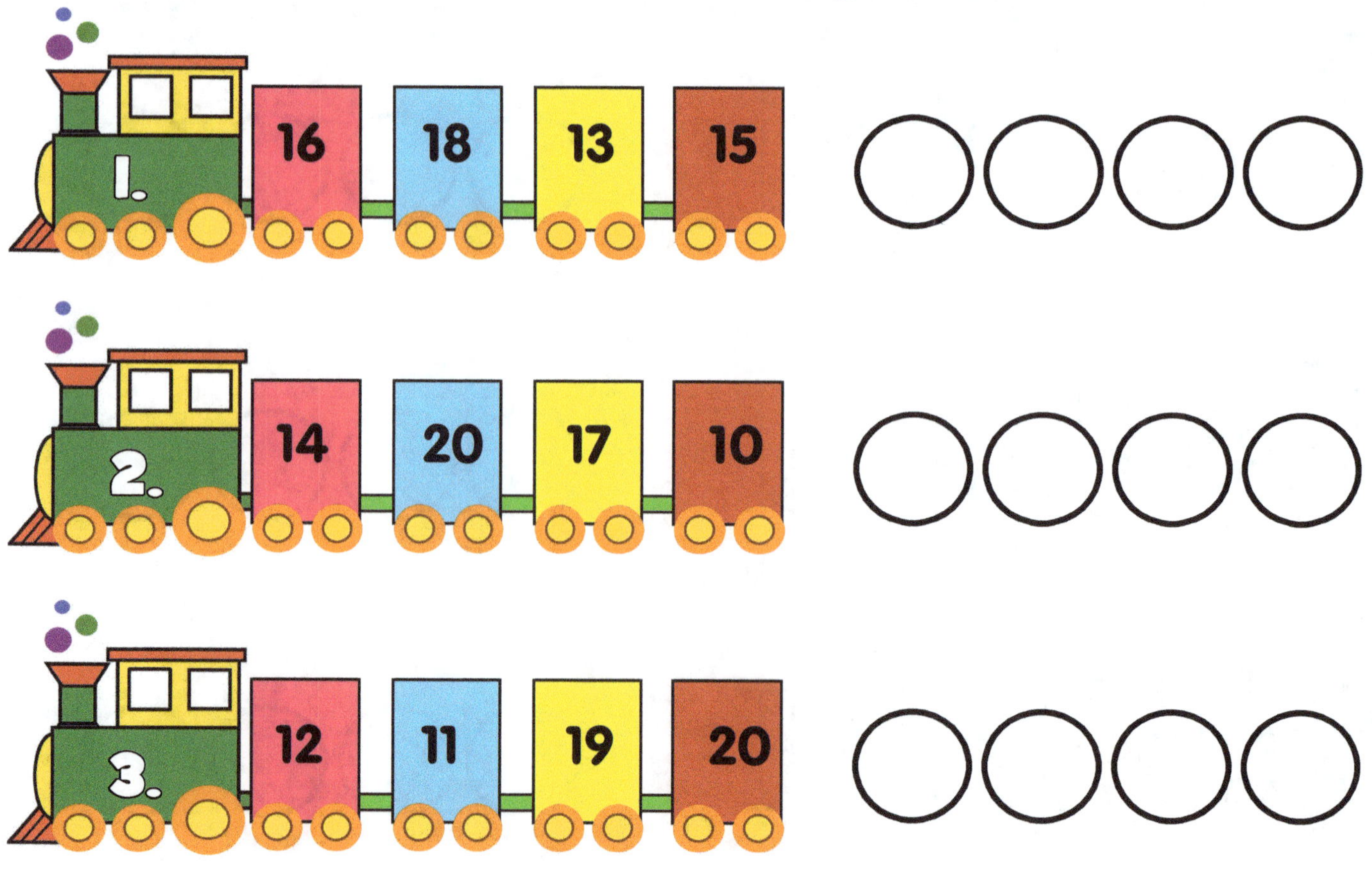

Name:______________________________ Score: __________

Arrange and write 8

123

Write the numbers from greatest to least.

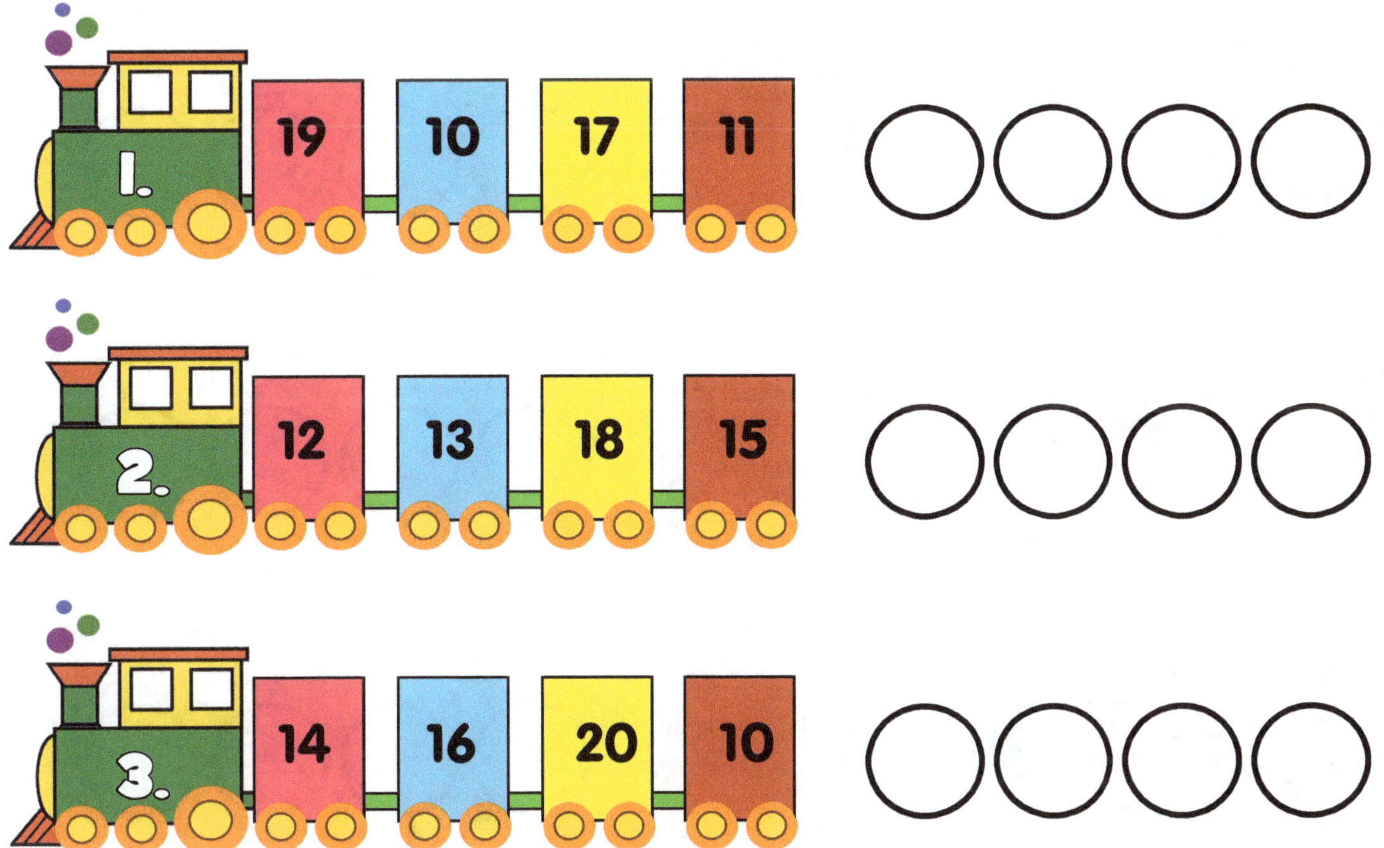

Name:______________________________ Score: __________

Arrange and write 9

Write the numbers from greatest to least.

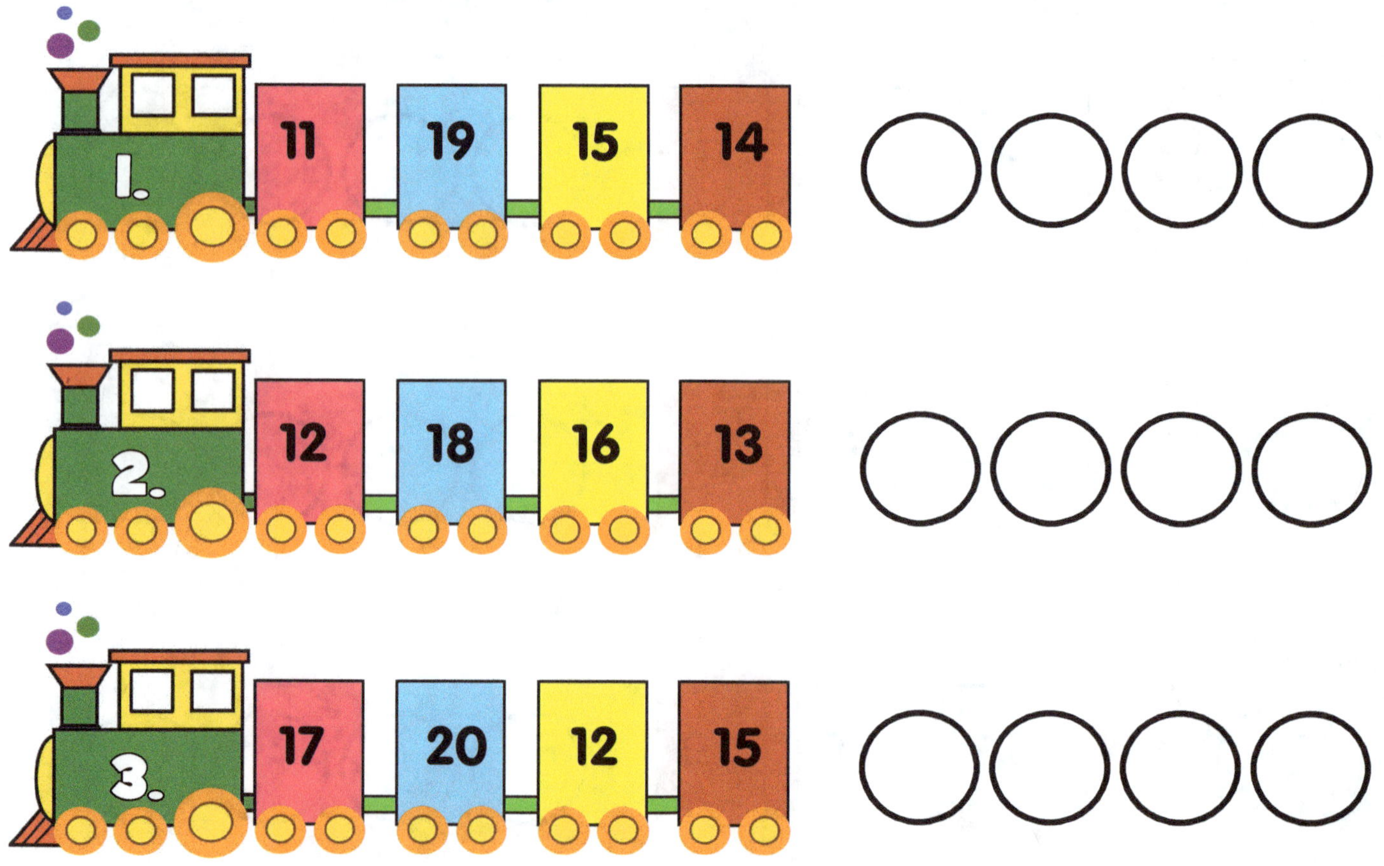

Name:______________________________ Score: __________

Arrange and write 10

Write the numbers from greatest to least.

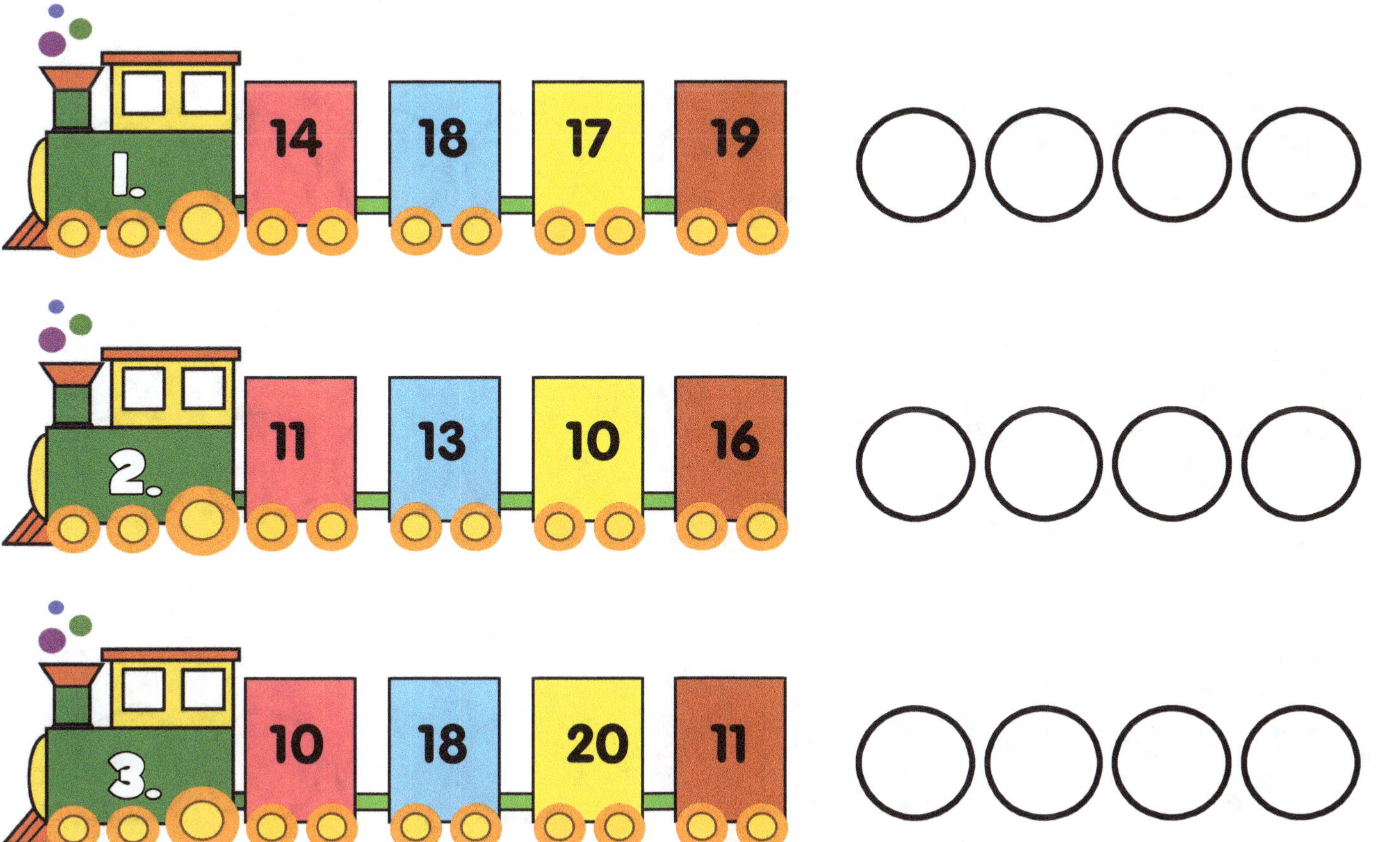

Name:______________________________ Score: __________

Arrange and write 11

Write the numbers from greatest to least.

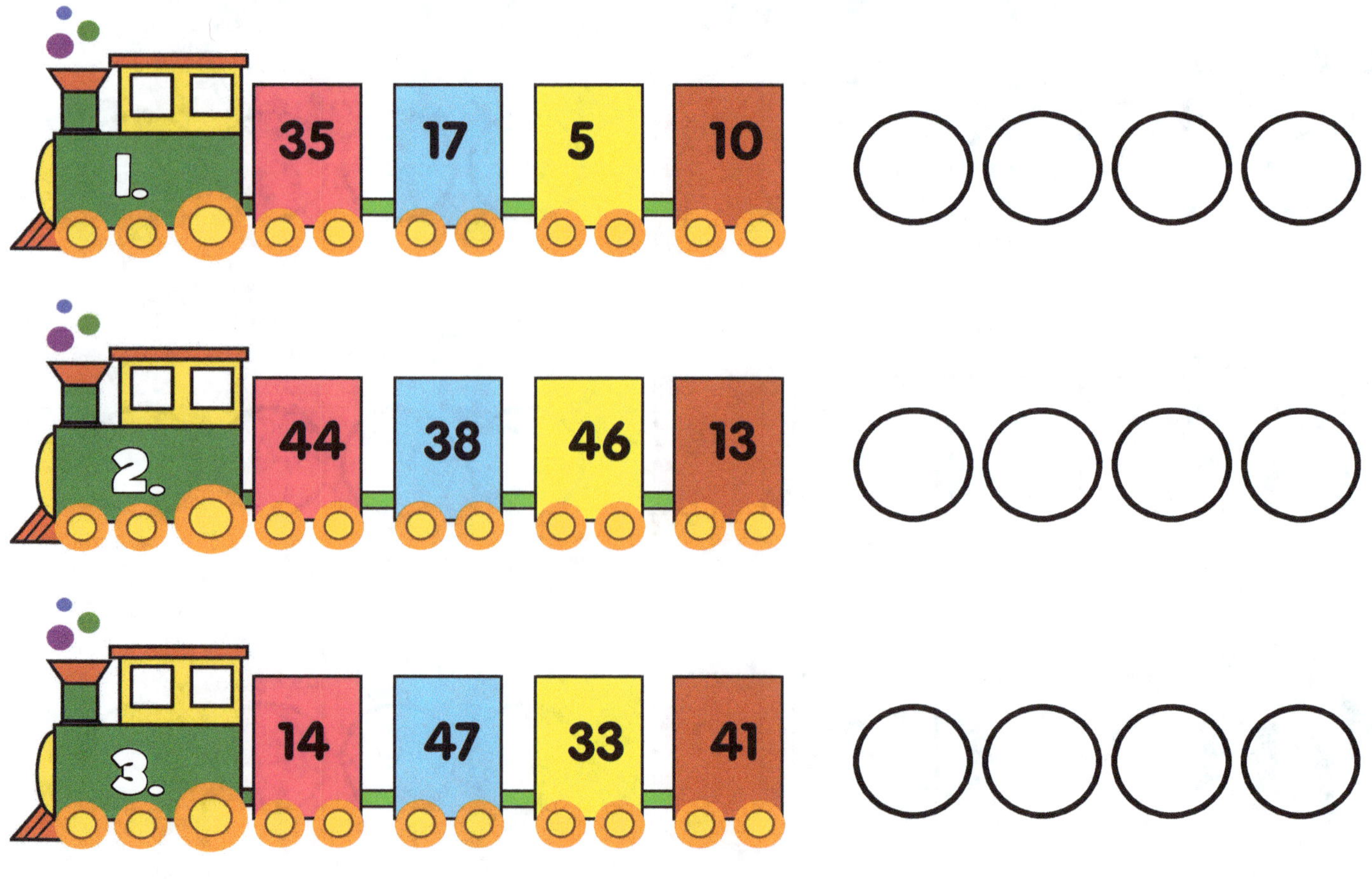

Name:________________________________ Score: __________

Arrange and write 12

Write the numbers from greatest to least.

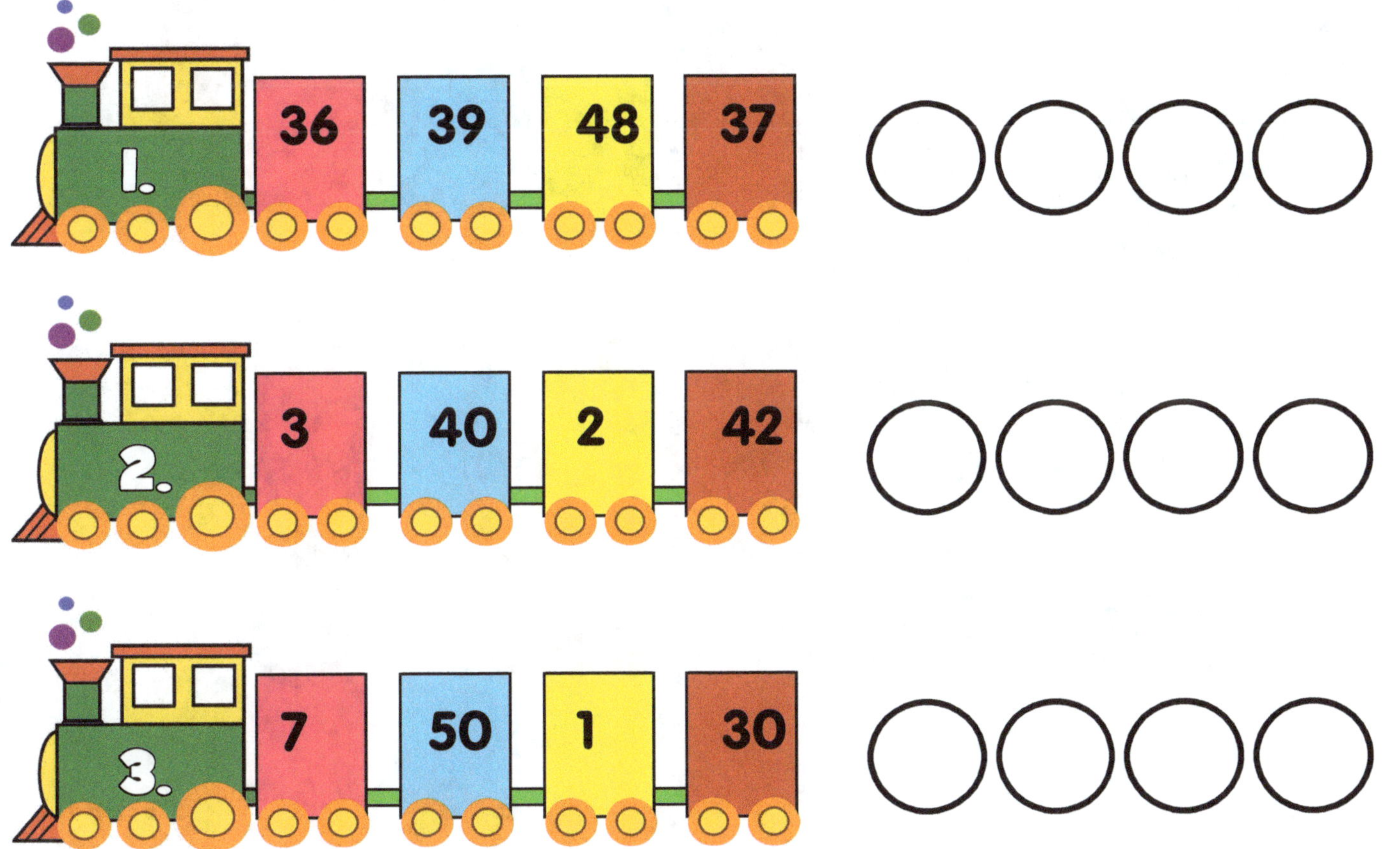

Name:______________________ Score: __________

GOOD
JOB!

Ascending

Cut and Paste 1

A. **10, 18, 19, 20**

B. **11, 12, 13, 15**

Cut and Paste 2

A. **12, 14, 16, 17**

B. **11, 14, 15, 18**

Cut and Paste 3

A. **13, 16, 17, 20**

B. **10, 13, 14, 19**

Cut and Paste 4

A. **10, 15, 19, 20**

B. **12, 16, 17, 18**

Cut and Paste 5

A. **10, 11, 16, 18**

B. **11, 13, 17, 19**

Cut and Paste 6

A. **12, 14, 15, 20**

B. **11, 14, 15, 16**

Cut and Paste 7

A. **5, 14, 18, 20**

B. **1, 2, 9, 16**

Cut and Paste 8

A. **3, 4, 6, 15**

B. **7, 8, 10, 11**

Cut and Paste 9

A. **12, 13, 17, 19**

B. **4, 10, 11, 16**

Descending

Cut and Paste 10

A. 18, 13, 12, 11

B. 17, 16, 15, 14

Cut and Paste 11

A. 20, 19, 13, 10

B. 18, 16, 12, 11

Cut and Paste 12

A. 19, 17, 15, 10

B. 20, 16, 14, 12

Cut and Paste 13

A. 18, 17, 13, 10

B. 20, 19, 14, 11

Cut and Paste 14

A. 17, 16, 15, 11

B. 20, 19, 18, 13

Cut and Paste 15

A. 15, 14, 12, 10

B. 18, 16, 12, 10

Cut and Paste 16

A. 13, 12, 6, 3

B. 16, 15, 14, 1

Cut and Paste 17

A. 19, 18, 17, 9

B. 20, 10, 5, 4

Cut and Paste 18

A. 11, 8, 7, 2

B. 20, 16, 6, 5

Arrange and Write 1

1. 22, 33, 38, 39
2. 4, 34, 44, 50
3. 7, 20, 27, 47

Arrange and Write 2

1. 10, 12, 23, 40
2. 11, 13, 21, 48
3. 24, 28, 41, 49

Arrange and Write 3

1. 1, 2, 5, 45
2. 16, 26, 36, 42
3. 14, 15, 25, 35

Arrange and Write 4

1. 17, 18, 31, 43
2. 3, 19, 29, 46
3. 6, 8, 9, 37

Arrange and Write 5

1. 3, 9, 33, 49
2. 15, 18, 20, 45
3. 17, 22, 42, 46

Arrange and Write 6

1. 6, 10, 12, 24
2. 11, 13, 23, 25
3. 14, 26, 27, 29

Arrange and Write 7

1. 18, 16, 15, 13
2. 20, 17, 14, 10
3. 20, 19, 12, 11

Arrange and Write 8

1. 19, 17, 11, 10
2. 18, 15, 13, 12
3. 20, 16, 14, 10

Arrange and Write 9

1. 19, 15, 14, 11
2. 18, 16, 13, 12
3. 20, 17, 15, 12

Arrange and Write 10

1. 19, 18, 17, 14
2. 16, 13, 11, 10
3. 20, 18, 11, 10

Arrange and Write 11

1. 35, 17, 10, 5
2. 46, 44, 38, 13
3. 47, 41, 33, 14

Arrange and Write 12

1. 48, 39, 37, 36
2. 42, 40, 3, 2
3. 50, 30, 7, 1

www.ingramcontent.com/pod-product-compliance
Lightning Source LLC
LaVergne TN
LVHW060827170826
845678LV00010B/1918
9798869442000